MW01003124

ANSCHEL'S STORY
DETERMINED TO SURVIVE

Renate Frydman

Dedication

I dedicate this book in loving memory of my late husband
Anschel (Charlie) Frydman.

And to all of our beloved family members
who perished in the Holocaust.

May We Always Remember. Educate. Heal.

Cover illustration by Randy Palmer.

Printed in the United States of America

First printing, 2017

Hard cover: ISBN 978-1-945091-49-0
Soft cover: ISBN 978-1-945091-64-3

Library of Congress Control Number: 2017959849

Ordering information: Special discounts are available on quantity purchases by bookstores, corporations, associations, and others. For details, contact the publisher at:

sales@braughlerbooks.com
or at 937-58-BOOKS

For questions or comments about this book, please write to:

info@braughlerbooks.com

Braughler™
Books
braughlerbooks.com

Table of Contents

Foreword

On the eve of the Second World War, Poland had a Jewish population of approximately 3.3 million. Barely 400,000 survived the Nazi genocide, most of them in the Soviet Union and many did not return to post-war Poland. According to the records of the Central Committee of Jews in Poland *(Centralny Komitet Żydów w Polsce—CKŻP)* the principal Jewish body in post-war Poland, 74,000 people had registered with it by June 1945. Of these 5,500 had returned from concentration camps in Germany, 13,000 had served in the pro-communist Polish Army established in the USSR after the withdrawal of the Anders Army, about 30,000 had made their way back from the Soviet Union, 10,000 had been freed from concentration camps in Poland and the remainder had survived on the 'Aryan side'. Some, who had survived on 'aryan papers' did not return to the Jewish community. In the next two years more than 136,000 Jews returned from the USSR, mostly people who had been deported or evacuated to the interior of the country. By 1 July 1946, nearly 244,000 Jews had registered with the CKŻP. Men survived the war more successfully than women--at this time the ratio of men to women was 54.3 per cent to 45.7 per cent.

One of those who survived is Anschel Frydman, the voice of this remarkable and moving memoir. His story is a microcosm of the tragic fate of Polish Jews during the Shoah. Born in the small town of Jedlińsk, he was 11 when the Nazis invaded Poland and describes the devastating impact of their occupation, first on his native town and then on Warsaw, where he was sent by his father to take food to his uncle and two aunts who had been confined in the ghetto established there in October 1940. His father, mother and two sisters were all murdered and he survived, first by finding shelter in the countryside with Poles and Volksdeutsche and then as a slave labourer in the labour camp at the ammunition factory of Pionki. He was able to escape from this camp and join the People's Army (Armia Ludowa), the pro-communist underground force which was in bitter conflict with the larger Home Army (Armia Krajowa), linked with the Polish government in London. He shows clearly why it was very difficult for Jews to join this latter force. He also gives, through the eyes of an intelligent teenager, a nuanced picture of the relations between Poles and Jews in the countryside, where some of the majority community were prepared to aid their Jewish fellow citizens while others assisted the Nazis in their genocidal plans.

Anschel survived the war only to confront anti-Jewish threats in his native town of Jedlińsk to which he returned which led him to flee to Germany. He eventually made his way to the United States where he married Renate, who persuaded him to record his memories. Together they had four children and ten grandchildren. Anschel is no longer alive, but this memoir is a tribute to his indomitable spirit, emblematic of the Jews of Poland. It deserves the widest possible audience.

—*Antony Polonsky*

Emeritus Professor of Holocaust Studies,
Brandeis University

Chief Historian,
POLIN Museum of the History of Polish Jews, Warsaw

Preface

Many people have asked questions about survivors of the Holocaust in Europe. Why did one person live through the brutality and murder of millions and others did not? As in any event of this magnitude, there are more questions than answers.

I first met Anschel at a wedding of recently arrived survivors that my mother requested I attend. Anschel had also just arrived in this country and was at the wedding. I was a teenager in high school and he was a twenty-two year old survivor of the Holocaust. He spoke some English; though Polish, Yiddish, and German were his main languages.

From the beginning, even that first night when he asked me out, he told me stories of his early life, his home, his losses and what he went through. It came out in bits and pieces over two years' time. I was a writer/journalist, but I was too intrigued to write down the stories then. I just listened attentively. I was as fascinated with this handsome young man as he seemed to be taken with me.

After dating on and off for a year, it was obvious that we were in love. He asked me to marry him and in 1953 we were married. In the next eight years, we had four children. Having a home and family meant the world to him. The years were busy. He was working very hard to make a living. I was taking care of the family and working part time. He told our young children very little of what had happened to him. He didn't want to traumatize them. They heard little fragments of his early life and about some of his escapes from captivity.

Then one day, on a long road trip thirty years into our marriage, I brought out my tape recorder. I asked him to tell me something about his years of survival. Parts of the story poured out.

For twenty more years, whenever it seemed right, I pulled out the recorder and there was more of the story. A couple of tapes were recorded when I could coax him to speak at a school with me. I was a frequent speaker on the Holocaust for many years and still am today. He wasn't sure young people would understand. Yet, somehow as they listened quietly, they did.

A total of nine tapes were made and stored. I had hoped that he and I could write the story together one day. Then, in 2004, he passed away suddenly. I was left with the tapes that I couldn't listen to for seven more years. The sound of his voice tore me apart. To pull myself together, I remembered what it had taken for him to survive. He had given me the tools. I just needed to use them.

So, I took out one tape at a time and began transcribing them in long-hand. The story filled an entire notebook. The difficult part was to combine all the tapes into one cohesive story. With the patient assistance of my youngest daughter, Melinda, who typed every word on the computer as I read, this book slowly developed.

It is the true story of one teenager whose quest to survive continued even after the loss of all his close family members, his home, and everything dear to him. He fought to live on in spite of ghettos, fatal line-ups, brutality, enslavement in Nazi work camps, being surrounded by barbed wire, and, finally, years of survival in thick and endless forests that stretched for hundreds of miles.

Anschel's Story: Determined to Survive is a heart stopping journey told in first person, which describes unusual courage and uncanny luck. Now, thirty years after making the first recording, his story is ready to be shared. It will forever be engraved on our memory.

Acknowledgements

In many ways, this book has been in process for over thirty years. Beginning with the twenty years I was able to audio tape Anschel from time to time, until he passed away suddenly in 2004, I had hoped to write the story of his extraordinary life with him beside me.

When that was no longer possible, it took seven more years until I could listen to the tapes and transcribe them. Each time I heard the remarkable events of his teenage years, I became more convinced that this was a story that needed to be read by a wider audience than just my family.

Now, six years after beginning to set the story on the computer, I am ready to give it to the world. My hope is that those reading Anschel's resolve to survive will look for that strength and resiliency inside themselves.

Without the following people, I would have struggled much longer. It is with deep gratitude and appreciation that I list those who assisted me the most. They never wavered in their belief that this book of Anschel's story showed the courage, determination, and resilience of the human spirit that is a unique example of survival.

My Family

I am most thankful to my four children and their spouses who encouraged me throughout this long process. They are joined by my ten grandchildren who keep telling me how anxious they are to read the whole book.

My youngest daughter, Melinda, sat by my side all those years typing her father's transcribed words as I read them. She took this task very seriously as she knew she was keeping her beloved father's important memories alive for her children, our family, and many other readers. Often as she typed, she stopped breathless at her father's daring and fortitude in the face of perilous odds.

Charlotte, my daughter, kept us on track with words of encouragement. She edited the manuscript's spaces, punctuation, and paragraphs over and over as we moved along, with a trained eye and a full heart.

Farley, my son, introduced us to Professor Antony Polonsky who he knew from Brandeis University, his alma mater. Farley provided constant inspiration and support to keep us going.

Joel, my son, never stopped prodding us to continue working on the story. An attorney, he was our expert in certain matters. He also brought back his remembrances of his father's stories and it was of utmost importance to him that the book become a reality.

My son-in-law, Bill, who made himself available to fix every computer glitch I managed to create.

My Colleagues

Professor Antony Polonsky, a world-renowned expert on Poland with twenty-nine books to his credit on that country's history, stayed with the project throughout the years. An incredible person of patience and knowledge, his advice has been invaluable in many aspects of the historical background and locations of Anschel's manuscript.

Dr. Thomas Martin, Professor Emeritus of History and Humanities at Sinclair College, and long-time right hand to my Holocaust programs, was never too busy to listen and motivate me. His keen research helped me keep the story in accurate perspective.

Rosemarie Meyer, a retired teacher, writer, editor and Holocaust Education Committee member, read and endorsed the original manuscript.

Allen Seymour has been my sounding board during this process. He listened, sometimes tearfully, as I read the chapters of the story, and creatively helped me choose the title and cover best suited to the book.

My sincere thanks to my publisher, David Braughler, for his patience and assistance.

I am extremely grateful to Katrina Kittle, an author and my extraordinary editor.

Also to Randy Palmer, artist and illustrator, who designed and labored over the cover of this book, I appreciate his huge talent and vision.

Renate Frydman
November, 2017

Anschel's Story

The year was 1942

I was running into the forest, I don't know how long. I ran and ran. I don't know if I ran ten miles or fifteen. I just kept running and running until I fell asleep in the forest. But when I woke up, it was dawn, almost a day gone. I must have fallen down and fallen asleep for a whole day. I was knocked out.

When I woke up, it was dark again and I wanted to get away. I kept walking and running, and running and walking for most of the night until I got tired again, because I wanted to get as far away from that place, Pionki, as possible. I couldn't go anymore. I had no idea where I was. I was alone.

Anschel's cousin Pinkwas, leaning on Jedliński town sign after the war.

CHAPTER ONE

Jedlińsk

Jedlińsk, Poland was chartered in 1530 and is today a town of 1,700 people about nine miles north of the larger city of Radom and forty-nine miles from Warsaw. The name derives from the Polish jodła, "fir tree." Before the war, it had a large Jewish population, dating back at least to the eighteenth century. In 1921, Jews were half the population. When the Germans occupied the town, a ghetto was established; that ghetto was liquidated, the Jews forced out, in August 1942. Those not killed on the spot were transported to Treblinka.

I was born in a small town in Poland called Jedlińsk in 1928. We were a family of five: my parents, Chana and Joseph Chaim, my two younger sisters, Chaya and Ruchu, and me. We had a little farm and as a small boy I milked the cows in the morning and we lived a nice, quiet life. There was one small synagogue *(shtibel)* in my town and along the street were little houses.

It was an idyllic life, unmarred by material demands, just day to day living. Families were often large, neighbors

Anschel's father. This is the only picture of Anschel's father in the world.

Anschel's mother, Chana, taken to Treblinka Death Camp at age 30 with her two younger daughters.

Young Anschel in his hometown around 11 years old. Before the War.

visited frequently and the outside world seemed far away. An occasional rowdy gang appeared, often after church on Sunday, looking for fights with the Jews. Yet, there were business contacts, such as a Jewish butcher selling parts of

This is a picture of some of Anschel's male family members, taken in early 1930's and sent to cousins in Brazil. His father, Joseph, is the second man on the left. The cousin that he stayed with in the Radom Ghetto is the first man on the left next to Joseph. His name was Haswolle. The man with the white beard was Anschel's grandfather's brother. Everyone in the picture, including the two children, was killed in the Holocaust. Two of the men, brothers, Haswolle and Haskell, survived.

slaughtered cattle forbidden for Jews to eat to a Christian butcher. There was bartering of produce, livestock, and other goods in the weekly markets. However, there was not much actual socializing between the ethnic groups.

My father's side of the family lived in Białobrzegi. My mother's side all lived in Jedlińsk. My mother's father, my grandfather, was very well off. My father had little money and he worked for his father-in-law. In summer, my father leased a big fruit farm from a land baron. He worked at the butcher store, except for the summers when he worked on the fruit farm. We lived on the fruit farm in the summer. My father built a small house there like a barn. He built beds and he built his own oven. It always smelled fresh there. We had all kinds of fruit: berries, cherries, apples, plums and pears. The fruit was delicious!

We had farm hands to help with the fruit picking and my mother cooked for them. They ate outside on a long table. It was wonderful there in the orchard.

I always wanted a bike. There was a big market each year in my town. They sold things and had festivals. My father knew many farmers and they parked their bikes in our backyard when they went to market for the day. The bikes had stirrups on the pedals. I took one of the bikes and tried to ride it. The bike kept going faster and faster downhill. Soon, I made a big crash into the wooden fence! The front wheel of the bike was smashed and looked like a figure eight. I knew the guy who owned the bike was going to kill me. Someone said, "you are in big trouble." My mother took me into town to a guy who fixed bikes. He took out the spokes and put in new spokes. We put the bike back and it was like nothing had happened.

We had a peaceful life. Yet, it was hard and we had our troubles and our problems with Polish kids. We knew there was anti-Semitism. School was two blocks from my house and was from 8:00 am to 3:00 pm. For lunch, I took an apple, an egg sandwich, and tea. After school, we went to a private school which continued with a Jewish teacher to study my schoolwork. Some days, I would ride my bike to the *Rebbe's* (rabbi's) house, which was right across the street for Hebrew lessons. No question—no other way. At fourteen you were done with school and you went to work with your father or to *yeshiva* (orthodox Jewish school). On Sundays, the Polish people were all stirred up when they came out of church. One wealthy man came out of church and liked to throw rocks at the windows of Jewish homes. The next day he would feel bad and paid for new windows to be put in.

We lived in a double house and one half belonged to us. My grandmother started on Thursday morning to bake for the Sabbath. We had plenty of fish because there were fish ponds three kilometers from our town. There were different kinds of fish: carp, *hecht,* and white fish. The river by our town was a tributary of the Vistula River, which was so clean you could drink from it. On Friday morning, my mother made a *Challah* bread, *Gefilte* Fish and sponge cakes for every Sabbath. If you didn't have fish for Friday night in the house, it was terrible. You couldn't cook on Saturday, so on Friday my mother prepared a big pot of *cholent* (beef stew). It had beef ribs, potatoes, carrots, and beans. I took the pot covered with a lid and paper around it, tied up, to the bakery. It cooked all night in a hot brick oven and the next day, I took the pot home for dinner.

The main thing the wife had to do was to take care of the family and be good in the house. She had to have large quantities of potatoes, flour, salt, and eggs. Someone milked the cow and they made butter. I went to the bakery every morning to bring fresh bagels, always fresh from that day.

When I was young, we had no plumbing. We went to a well right by us, near a little river going through. I took two-gallon buckets and (sometimes) I fell over with the buckets so I had to get another bucket of water. I chopped wood and we stocked it away for winter. I dumped coal in a hole in the cellar with a little door. Life was very hard. We didn't know anything else.

The open farmland started to freeze late in December and there were miles and miles of ice. We put on ice shoes so we could walk through the yard. I fell in the ice water and it all froze on me! My father was really, really angry and spanked me. My mother always protected me.

My cousin Henry lived across the street and I was in his house as much as my house. You knew everybody in town. Ethel and Nathan Weisman lived in the second house from us in Jedlińsk. We often went there and had tea and peanuts and were singing songs. My mother read many books and talked about the plight of German Jews. We felt sorry for them.

Life in Poland was tough. People wanted

Henry after War when he came to Dayton.

to make a better life. Some left to go to other countries. My mother's two first cousins, Elke and Moishe, went to Brazil in the early 1930's. When the war broke out, my father wanted to leave. His suitcase was packed and he was ready to go. My mother and we kids were crying. My father gave up. There was nowhere to go. Where would you go from Poland? In September of 1939, the war broke out. The storm clouds started to gather. The German troops came through Poland from one side and the Russian troops from the other side. Immediately, we felt there was trouble when the war broke out. Trouble started right away with the Jewish people.

The Molotov-Ribbentrop Pact, signed in Moscow on August 23, 1939, was a neutrality pact between Nazi Germany and the Soviet Union. It described the spheres of interest between the two powers. It was amended after the joint invasion of Poland. A secret codicil to the Molotov-Ribbentrop pact, called the German-Soviet Frontier Treaty, was signed in late September 1939. It made some adjustments to the new German-Soviet border, especially involving Lithuania, and also concerned the exchange of prisoners.

The Germans and Russians had made a pact. The Polish army did not have many tanks and very few airplanes. It didn't take long for the Germans and Russians to take Poland. Each got half.

I was in Jedlińsk when the German army went through, right in the middle of Poland, not far from Warsaw. It did not take long for the Germans to take over all of Warsaw, the capital of Poland.

First they took control of the leaders of the city and killed many of them. Residents had to register every-thing—name, age, even livestock like cows and horses.

In my town, they made ten people responsible to see that everyone registered. You had to give your radios to the Germans. There were no more schools, no newspa-pers. Everything stopped.

As they started making trouble with the Jews, they were taking the people to work. People were ordered to do this work and that, but there really wasn't anything to do. It was just to keep us busy. The Polish police immedi-ately went over to sympathize with the Germans.

There were a lot of people living in parts of Poland whose parents were from Germany. They could speak both Polish and German. There were almost a million such people, and they were very, very dangerous. They knew in each town everybody who was Jewish, who was Polish, and who was a gypsy. These Polish Germans put an arm band on with a German swastika, and they were now German. That's how it was.

Things got worse by the day, every day. But we man-aged, because there was no luxury in Poland. We were all poor. We managed somehow to live. There were no mov-ies to go to in our town, no special places. We were used to this simple kind of life, but after the Germans came in, things got very bad.

There were airplanes flying very low and they were shooting everything that moved. Children, women, men, it did not make any difference. They were shooting all day, every day. People were afraid to be outside.

The Germans could do whatever they wanted to with you and your family. It didn't matter if you were Polish or Jewish. And if they wanted to eliminate you on the spot, they could do it. There was no law and there was no court.

Finally, a week later, as I was living in the part where the German troops went through, things got really bad. Day after day there were new signs—they made people 16 to 60 go out to work. I went to work so my father didn't have to go. They just made us go with shovels and clean and then cover up the holes, for doing nothing wrong. But, we did everything they asked us to do.

They took out leaders from my town, like the priest, they took the rabbi, four teachers, and the principal of the school, and two or three from the Polish committee. Except for the rabbi, all the others were not Jewish. They killed them, all ten. They took them away, about seven kilometers from the town, into a little forest and killed them all, for no reason—that's it.

Every single night there was shooting. You could hear the screams and killings night after night. Every day there was something new going on like that.

Somehow, we managed. I was young and strong and if you worked, they gave you a little bread or something. I was able to bring home a little something to eat for my family. They depended on me to supply them with food in order to live.

When the war broke out on September 1, 1939, and Germany declared war on Poland, they gave out tickets in our town. The tickets meant you would go immediately that day to the Army. My grandfather was very excited, very nervous, because we were a large family and some of them got those tickets. I don't know if they were red or green tickets, I believe they were green.

My grandfather was running around to find out who had been given the tickets. When he was crossing the main highway, a car with Polish officers was in a hurry to go to Radom. The car hit him. They broke his leg and we kept him a few days at home and we could not give him a lot of help.

So, finally my mother rented a car and driver and they took him to Warsaw to a hospital. She came back the following day. But a week later the Germans were already in our town. That's how quickly they went through Poland. But Warsaw went on fighting for another three weeks.

Meanwhile, we could not get to my grandfather because the war was going on in Warsaw. We didn't know anything about what was happening to him for a long time, three or four more weeks. When the battle was over, my mother paid a *Wehrmacht* (German Armed Forces soldier) a lot of money to take her and another guy to Warsaw.

They found my grandfather in the hospital and he was lying under a blanket and covered up completely with glass. The hospital had been bombed. He did not recognize my mother and the doctors said they could not help him much there. They said to take him home.

There was no medicine available, so they took him back to Radom to a hospital, but a doctor said it was too late. They could not save him anymore. He had already developed gangrene. A few days later, he passed away.

Also, my mother's first cousin's son and another cousin of my mother's were carrying tomatoes from a farm that was three kilometers from our town. The German airplanes were flying all over shooting and bombing. They must have seen the red tomatoes on the highway. One of the cousins got killed and the other was wounded very badly. Our family was one of the first to suffer immediately. Right away, we had casualties when the war broke out.

The Germans had us surrounded. Poland thought they were prepared, they thought they were going to beat the hell out of the Germans. They were so sure. We had horses and all kinds of weapons. But the flyers were shooting the horses right on the way. The Poles had nothing but bicycles and horses, and a few small tanks. Poland had airplanes, but they were not good. They were older types of planes.

One day, in the morning, there was a neighbor who was an older man. His son was living with him. The father was a very, very rich man, dealing with corn, flour, sugar, and salt. He had a little store that sold candies. That was a big thing in Poland. He had his own house and his own store and the Poles must have told the Germans about him and they took him out of his home.

Our dog ran out of the house and was barking at the German police and a German took out a pistol and shot our dog. Then they took away this old man and we found out they took him less than a mile away. They made him dig his own grave and shot him by the side of a bridge on the highway.

We lived in this small town, and we couldn't go to the synagogue anymore, so the *torahs* (holy scrolls) were given to different families. We were approached if we could take a *torah*. They asked people who had more than one room.

We had a kitchen in our house and when you came in to the left, there was a room and from this room it went into another room. My parents accepted the *torah* and every Saturday morning they had services. I had my *Bar Mitzvah* in my own house.

On the Sabbath, people walked in secretly from the neighborhood and they made a *minyan* (congregational quorum of 10 adult men). Some relatives came in. There was always a *minyan*, more than ten. But they could not come in bunches. They had to keep quiet, come in slowly, one by one. They could not make a tumult so suspicion would not be aroused that something was going on, like holding secret services, which were forbidden.

They *davened* (prayed) the evening prayers, the *minhah* and *ma'ariv*. The *torah* was hidden in that room. We had a big *shrank* (a wardrobe closet). It had three or four doors we could open up so it was solid inside. We moved the *shrank* so you could not see the doors. On Saturday mornings, we pushed away the *shrank* and people moved around it. When the service was over, we moved it back so it looked like nothing was there.

We lived in three rooms and a kitchen. There was a porch used only for the high holidays and we sat and ate there like in a *sukkah* (a booth).

In the end of 1939, my father was still there. There were different towns around close by. In one of the towns, the Germans moved out all the people—Jews and Poles had to leave. We had to take families into our town. The Jewish community walked around and would see who could give up a room.

Przytyk is a village in east-central Poland founded in 1333. It lies twelve miles west of Radom and fifty-two miles south of Warsaw. In 2006 it had a population of 990 persons. Przytyk was the scene of an anti—Semitic pogrom March 7-9, 1936. Prior to the Holocaust, some 80% of population of the village was Jewish. Most perished in the Holocaust. In March 1941, Przytyk and the surrounding areas turned into a Luftwaffe training facility. All Polish residents were ordered to leave the village, and all buildings were destroyed by the Germans. As a result, there are no historic buildings in Przytyk.

My parents agreed to take in one family from another town called *Przytyk*. This town, before the war, had one of the biggest pogroms in the history of Poland. After

1936, it became world renowned. A number of Jews got killed, as well as some Poles got killed by the Jews. Many people were killed that day.

A family with a horse and buggy came in a couple days later to my town. Instead of one family there were two families. There was a mother, father, two sons and a daughter. One son was married and he had one child. They all lived in one room. They were happy to have a roof over their heads.

In the night, they laid out blankets and slept on them. They shared and cut up bread and my mother made potato soup and whatever she had that they could eat. All of the men were shoemakers and they were sitting making shoes, fixing shoes, whatever they could do for five or six months.

CHAPTER TWO

The Warsaw Ghetto

The Nazi invasion of Poland took place in September 1939 and by October 1940 they had confined nearly 400,000 Jews in a 3.5 square mile area of Warsaw. It had previously housed about 160,000 persons. The area was surrounded by a ten foot wall and was sealed off on November 15, 1940. Jews were forbidden to go outside the area on penalty of being shot on sight. They had no further contact with the outside world. The Nazis refused to allow enough food to

be brought into the ghetto to keep Jews healthy. They were forced to survive on as little as a bowl of soup a day. Three to four hundred persons died each day from starvation and disease. By July 1942, about 80,000 Jews had perished.

In July 22, 1942, upon orders from Reichsführer Heinrich Himmler, a massive "resettlement" as the Nazis called it, took place of Jews taken out of the ghetto. They were sent to be gassed in Nazi extermination camps, mainly Treblinka. In just two months, 310,322 Jews were sent to their deaths.

My father had a brother and two sisters in Warsaw. It was 90 kilometers from Jedlińsk. It had gotten so bad in the ghetto. A letter got through somehow, not by mail, that his sister and her two children were starving. There was no food and they had nothing.

I remember, I snuck into the ghetto late in 1940. My parents decided to fix some food up for me to take to Warsaw. But you could not travel easily. All Jewish people had to wear a Star of David on the left arm sleeve. But, I was blond and did not look Jewish. So, I got out without the star.

My parents packed up two suitcases with the food and I managed to get up very early in the morning. It was still dark and I walked about a mile to the main highway. I stopped a German *Wehrmacht* truck. I waved them down. I said "Warsaw" and they said "yes" they were going to Warsaw. The Germans did not know I was Jewish.

You had to have a little bit of guts to do things and I did! I had all the instructions from my father, what to do when I got to Warsaw. The truck stopped and I was in Warsaw with my two suitcases. I got off and took my suitcases and took a certain electric train *(a trumvei or tramwajowy in Polish)* that went through the Warsaw Ghetto.

The Germans did not have much choice, because trains went through certain streets and they couldn't change everything. The trolley drove through the ghetto pretty fast. When I saw the Jews living in the ghetto, I threw the suitcases off and jumped down. Somehow I managed to get to our family's house and brought them the food. When they saw me with the two suitcases of food, they were starving. It was like an angel had come down from heaven. They had no idea I was coming. When I was there, they were still okay, my aunt and uncle. They had lost a lot of weight. When I left, they cried a lot.

Now was the question, how to get out? I did not want to stay and eat their food, since I had to eat, too. The Germans raided the ghetto, took so many away and made the young people work. Every morning, the SS came. They needed 150 men to work. They put them on trucks and they were never heard from again. People died every day. There was no food and push carts were used to take bodies out and dump them into a big mass grave.

The conditions in the ghetto were just awful. What I have seen there, I wouldn't want to see that in my lifetime anymore. People were lying on the street, they were swollen. They were dying on the street by the dozens. Every minute you could see they were falling and there were pushcarts picking them up and taking them away by the cartload, not just one or two. It was *really* bad.

Getting out of the ghetto was not easy. Poles were sitting on the trolley car. And if you jumped on from the ghetto, the Poles told the Germans and they took you away. It was hard to get out and I was scared to death. I didn't know what to do.

My uncle found out you could get out through the Polish Police. You could pay them off. I found out that this Polish officer is there at a certain time and he looks away as you walk out to the other side through a revolving door. My uncle paid him off and five minutes later, I walked out through the revolving door. When you walk through the corridor, you were actually already out on the other side. I walked out past the Polish officer. He knew. I walked out on that street called Żelazna and that street took you to the Polish courts.

From there I got through and when I got to the other side, it was very scary because the Germans were walking around patrolling everything. I walked right through the Germans and because they did not suspect I was a Jew, I made it through.

I got out and I did the same thing exactly to go home. From Goriereska Street, I went to the same highway. There was a whole bunch of Poles sitting, waiting, and one said "Radom" when a truck pulled up and they said "Radom" and I was one of them, too. I went to the truck. I wore no arm patch. I went just like them. I was a Pole.

When the truck came three or four kilometers near my city, I knocked on the cab and I jumped off. I didn't want the people from my town to see me. They knew I was Jewish. I snuck through the fields somehow, through the back way. It was tough to get to my house. It wasn't easy, but somehow I got back.

That was a big thing I did. Already at that time, I had enough courage to do something. Not everybody had the guts to do it. At least I helped them. I imagine they had food for a week or ten days. I don't know what happened to them. I didn't see them anymore.

Cousin Pinkwas standing by his family home.

CHAPTER THREE

Family Torn Apart

In 1941, shortly after I returned from the Warsaw Ghetto, the Germans took my father away with a whole bunch of other people and I never saw him again. Among the people the Germans took were all the butchers, about 12 of them from my city. My father, then thirty-one years old, was taken with all those men to jail in Radom.

He was there for a few months. I found out after the war from a man who was a Jewish policeman, that he was then put on a transport to Treblinka.

Six months after he was taken away, the Germans made a ghetto in my small town. We were moved to the back part of my town and lived with some relatives. Jedlińsk was not a big ghetto and that did not last very long.

We were removed from our house on the main street. A few of the men that were friends of ours, came and took apart one of the buildings where we kept our livestock. My father had just built it, maybe two years before the war. We were able to take it apart and rebuild it quickly in two or three days. It was placed next to my mother's cousin's house. He lived in back and allowed us to attach it to his house. It was okay, not too bad. We had a pretty nice room. We had a stove over there and lived there until we got moved again.

CHAPTER FOUR

Białobrzegi

Białobrzegi dates from the fourteenth century, and was chartered as a town in 1540. As of 2011 the population was 10,410. It is located about thirty-seven miles south of Warsaw and thirty miles north of Radom. The Pilica River runs through the town and two important roads cross there. In early 1941 the Nazis established a ghetto, and by August, 1,850 Jews were interned there. The ghetto was liquidated in July 1943, and those not killed on the spot were sent to Treblinka.

It was later in 1941 that they took us away to Białobrzegi which was about twelve kilometers from my town. They did this so they could get people together to make a transport to Treblinka, a place where they gassed people.

We got a Polish farmer with a horse and buggy to take us and a few things, like our beds, and we moved to Białobrzegi. There, an aunt took us into her house. We lived with her for awhile and I was able to get out every day.

I registered with the Germans as they took young people out to work for them on the highway. I had worked at this particular place before for a few months. The

Germans came in with a few trucks and took the young people out to work with putting up telephone wires not far from the city.

At least, we could get out and not be in that ghetto every day. We could get some food and the trucks took us out in the morning and in the evening brought us back.

I worked in the kitchen and I got some food every day. By going to work, I could bring food back to my mother and sisters—a loaf of bread, a little bit of butter, a few eggs. I managed somehow and they depended on me to bring back something so they could live.

But this did not last very long. I estimate around three weeks. In the meantime, every single night, there were shootings and shootings. The German police went into homes and they took people out and they just killed people for no reason.

The next morning you could hear, "this family got shot and that family got killed". It was just terrible. You could hear the bullets in the night—killings and killings. We could hear screams and it could be next door neighbors. Every day they took twenty, thirty or as many as fifty people away and we never saw them again.

Then, one day, at about five o'clock one morning, we could hear all kinds of noises. The Polish police and Germans told all the Jews to come out of the homes and they were concentrated in one place in the middle of the city where there was a big empty place.

That was the morning when they took my mother, sisters, and me out. My younger sister was seven and my older sister was nine years old. My mother was 30 years old. It was August 1942.

Everyone had to run out and while we were running, the Germans were shooting into the crowd. People were falling down all over. It was like a massacre.

The purpose wasn't actually to kill everyone. It was to concentrate the people to take them to the trains. The trains were waiting to take them to Treblinka.

In that city, Białobrzegi, there wasn't actually a station. They had to make the people walk eight kilometers to the train station where the trains were waiting.

Chana, Anschel's mother

CHAPTER FIVE

Escaping and Hiding Begins

When we got to that place where the Germans had taken us, my mother saw a Jewish policeman who was somehow related to my father. His name was Benish.

Chana, his mother, had to make a quick decision that no parent ever would want to make. Which of her children had the best chance to survive this calamity? Her son, Anschel, was the oldest and strongest. The girls had to stay with her no matter what was coming.

My mother must have felt something terrible was happening and tried to save my life. The reason I got out was because my mother went to this Jewish policemen. She begged him to get me out on one of those trucks. "Take my son out of here. Put him on the truck," She demanded of him. She pushed this man to take me on the truck and he was able to do it. They were taking a bunch of 40 to 50 people out to work and I was able to get away on one of those trucks.

The same trucks were lined up there that took people to work every day. I imagine that they didn't know what was going on themselves. The truck left half an hour later and it was filled up. They were taking us to the same place that they did every day. After the truck passed through my town, *Jedlińsk*, it went over a little bridge by a cemetery and had to slow down.

I was very young, about fourteen, at that time. When the truck came to our town, it was late in the afternoon. As it had to slow down to go through that little bridge, I was able to jump off and escape into the cemetery.

I jumped off, even though there was a German with a rifle on that truck. The German guard didn't shoot because the people on the truck were packed solid like the ants, all standing up.

He didn't run after me and the truck didn't stop, it just kept going. It was late, late in the afternoon and I was hiding in the cemetery until dark.

The next day, I went back towards my town and went to a Polish family my parents and I knew very well. When the family saw me, they were trembling, they were scared. They didn't know what to do, but they kept me there for two or three days. They only had one room and they had two small children. They couldn't keep me there very long. They knew the punishment for hiding a Jew could be death for the whole family.

They somehow managed to go to a farmer nearby and talk to him. He took me into his barn. Since I was blond and had a light complexion, I didn't look Jewish, so I managed to stay with that family on the farm for three months. The farmer kept me with his five or six cows and a bunch of horses in the barn. Their son had gone to school with me. The boy didn't know I was in the barn. His parents were afraid he would tell the Germans.

The mother came in and brought me some hot milk and some cooked potatoes. She gave me whatever they could scrape together twice a day. One day, the farmer came in and said, "Look, it's getting very hard. It's getting very dangerous and you have to leave." I didn't know what to do, but I knew I had to do something. I found out they had a lot of Jewish people in the place called Radom ghetto.

Pniewy

Grójec Chynów

Bielsk
Duży Jasieniec

Błędów **Warka**

Magnuszew

Goszczyn

Grabów
nad Pilicą

Promna

Mogielnica Stromiec

Głowaczów

Nowe Miasto **Białobrzegi**
nad Pilicą **Wyśmierzyce** **Kozienice**

Siechów

Klwów Stara Błotnica

Radzanów Jedlińsk

Pionki Gniewoszów

Odrzywół Jastrzębia Garbatka-
Potworów Przytyk -Letnisko

Drzewica Zakrzew **RADOM** Jedlnia- Policzna
-Letnisko

Rusinów Gózd **Zwoleń**

Gielniów Wolanów Przyłęk

Wieniawa Tczów

Przysucha Kowala-Stępocina Kazanów

Borkowice Orońsko Chotcza-
Gowarczów -Józefów

Chlewiska Jastrząb Wierzbica Ciepielów

Stary **Iłża** **Lipsko**
Szydłowiec Mirów
gm. Mirów Rzeczniów Solec
nad Wisłą

Sienno

CHAPTER SIX

Radom Ghetto

Radom is a city in east-central Poland located 62 miles south of Warsaw on the Mieczna River. It had 219,703 inhabitants as of 2013. Its original settlement dates back to the eighth or ninth century with a location on the edge of a large wilderness. Up to the Second World War, Radom had a large Jewish population, as high as 39% according to a census of 1897. On September 8, 1939, Radom was captured by the Wehrmacht. The German occupiers carried out several executions of civilians. They set up the Radom Ghetto in March 1941 with a population of 34,000 Jews. Liquidation of the ghetto began in August 1942 and ended in July 1944. Most of the Jews perished at the Treblinka extermination camp.

About eight kilometers away from our town was Radom, a big city, with about 175,000 people. So I decided to go to the German civilian that I had worked for and knew very well. I told him what was going on and asked that he take me to Radom Ghetto eight kilometers away. I told him I had relatives there. I had the courage to go to his house in the evening and when he saw me, he almost fell down. He thought I was dead.

"I am here," I told him. "You see I am alive." The woman he lived with, who was not his wife, talked him into not harming me, to take me in.

So, he agreed to take me to Radom. He started his truck and he threw a tarpaulin over me and drove in the night the eight kilometers to the ghetto.

He backed up to the brick wall of the ghetto and I jumped over the wall and he drove away. That was the city of Radom, already a real ghetto, with so many blocks closed off.

My mother's first cousin, Haswolle, lived there in the ghetto and was a Jewish policeman. I was able to get there and he took me in. He took care of me and gave me food and clothes.

He took me down to a kitchen where people could go in and have some soup, all kinds of things, but nothing like a luxury. Just enough food so you did not walk around hungry.

When I was there for several days, things looked pretty bad. The Germans came in every night, and the next morning we could hear what was going on. There were killings in the night, people in this house and that house.

I got plenty to eat because of my cousin, but it bothered me a lot what was going on. I couldn't take it there because every day you heard new things—killings and killings.

I was living with my cousin in a house with a hiding place for families and children. If the police came in, all the families were hidden in that bunker and I was there several times, too.

Then one morning my cousin woke me up. Something strange was going on and he didn't know what it was. He thought the ghetto was surrounded again and they probably would make a transport to Treblinka.

Most of the people didn't know where they were going at that time. They only knew they were taken away to forced labor or something worse.

I asked my cousin what he could do for me. He was going to hide me in the bunker like he did for his family. I said, "no I want to get out."

Haswolle said, "Let's try it."

He put his Jewish policeman's uniform on and police hat and he took me out. We came to the gate where there were Germans over there and they just let us go through. He told them he was taking me to the public bath where the showers were and they said "okay" and just let us go through.

When we came to the Polish side, he kept on walking a block or two and he told me to keep walking straight. I kept walking and he went right and I went left. We separated and he went back to a different gate to the ghetto. I never saw him again until after the war.

I was on a certain street and I knew my way around because I had been there practically every second day when I was a little kid with my bicycle. I always rode into the bigger city.

I came to the main highway and there was a horse and buggy and the farmer was half asleep. I jumped on that little thing and I hitch hiked with him to a camp where I knew my cousin was working.

That day they took out seven hundred and fifty people. And they sent them to Treblinka to be gassed. Most people didn't make it, a handful, just a very few from the ghetto made it out to survive.

CHAPTER SEVEN

Wsola Camp

From there I went to a little place called Wsola. They were loading bombs there. This was a time when the war had broken out between Germany and Russia. In Wsola, they had a bunch of people at the small airport where they were loading those bombs. I was able to get to this little place and work there for about nine months.

This was where the *Luftwaffe* (German Air Force) was loading ammunition and bombs at this little airport. The planes kept coming back after bombing Russia and they were working when I got there.

I wanted to go there because it was not a concentration camp, not with barbed wire. It was open and was a working camp not far from the small airport.

On the other side, not far away, was another camp where they did something all together different. There were Jews working in the fields.

Wsola was close to our town. One Sunday morning, very bright and early in the morning, they made us get out of the barracks where we slept. We were surrounded by the Gestapo and Polish police and we were about 450 people—men, women and children. They made us make

two lines and then they surrounded us all around with machine guns, rifles and all kinds of other guns. There were some Ukrainians, some SS and gendarmes (police). We knew nothing good was going to come out of that.

When the barracks were all empty, they came in to check if everyone was out, if no one was hiding. They found some men who were sick on the beds and they immediately took them and had them dig their own graves. When they dug holes four or five foot deep, the guards killed them and they were buried right there.

When daylight came, this one German gendarme came up with a machine gun. He walked through the two lines, facing us and he split the lines, one to left and one to right. I was very close to the cutoff.

The one on the left, he made us go back into the barracks where we lived. The ones on the right, he left them standing there. There were men, women and children in the line. When we were inside the barracks, we could immediately see the machine guns go off.

Five minutes later they killed the men, women and children outside—every single one of them—every child, every woman, every man. They killed all of them. We knew it was not good for us.

At the same time this was going on, they closed the barrack doors and nailed the windows and doors shut. We figured they are going to set the wooden barracks on fire, which they had done before in different places. Everybody was crying, the little children and the women. It was terrible.

After that killing and putting us in the barracks, the next morning, Germans came with trucks and took us away to a town called Szydlowiec.

CHAPTER EIGHT

Szydlowiec

Szydlowiec is an urban-rural district in east-central Po-land. It is about 68 miles south of Warsaw. As of 2006, the total population was 19,290, both rural and urban.

Szydlowiec was a town where they made soft leather goods. It wasn't a big city. This was a good spot to bring all the Jewish people from this area, from the smaller towns, so they could make different transports to Treblinka from there. It was easier for them to have all the Jews concentrated in one place.

This killing went on all over, not just in my town. Eight kilometers from my town, was a little village called Batazir. There was a camp with a lot of Jewish people from *Jedlińsk*. There was also a train station there.

A fellow that escaped told me in Batazir they did things a bit differently than what they did to the Jewish people before. They put all of them in the barracks and when they opened up the barracks doors, they took ten to kill and ten on the trucks.

The Poles had dug a mass grave, a very big grave. As the Jews watched, they did not know what was going on.

Then, the Jews had to kneel down and the machine guns were set up and they were shooting and the Jews fell right into the hole. That's how terrible it was over there.

The Jews took one of the Germans and pulled him into the grave while the fighting was going on. While the one guy was holding the German, the other nine started to run. Germans were shooting after them immediately and one of them that I know escaped.

This also was in the forest, but the forest wasn't thick. The Germans cut a lot of trees around there where the barracks were. We all ended up in the same city the next day, whoever was alive from the little towns around.

So, the next morning, when they took us on the trucks to take us to Szydlowiec, other trucks also came up from other places. They parked right behind us. Yet, the Germans were still not satisfied with what they had done.

About two or three men from Jedliński, the Jewish community *Rada,* they took them off and took them to the side of the bridge and shot them, killed them right there as we watched. I knew every one of them, the people they shot. They were still blood-thirsty after they did so much killing.

Then the trucks took off to Szydlowiec, some right behind us. We were in front, a whole bunch of us who survived.

When I got there, I met some friends from different places when they came in and immediately I tried to see how I could escape. I looked around all day and found several other fellows who were ready to go.

By the next morning, we had six guys and in the evening about eleven o'clock, we escaped. We were running all night through an area where no civilian people were allowed. No Poles, nobody. It was strictly for the army, for the *Wehrmacht* and the Gestapo, a strictly military space.

But we ran all night through that area, and in the morning when it got light, we were hiding through the day under a bridge. There were five of us, because one man had kept going. He did not want to stop. He was my cousin and he left because his brother was in the work camp.

Only one guy had a gun. We were hiding under a bridge all day ten kilometers from my town. We had to be careful that no one could see us as the *Wehrmacht* camp was within sight.

We ran in the night to get away. We ran back in the direction of my town—back to *Jedlińsk*, my town, which was surrounded by fish ponds, where they raise fish.

At this time, they chose me and the one guy with a gun to go, when it got dark, to find a place for us to stay.

As we were on one side of the water, Germans with rifles were walking on the other side of the water. They saw us and told us we should stop! "Halt, halt," they shouted.

We didn't stop, just kept running. The Germans were on the other side of the water and we were on this side, and they were shooting at us. But they couldn't do anything. We ran away. We split up and I don't know what happened to the other guy. I never saw him again.

CHAPTER NINE

Hiding and Working

So, I gave up and returned three kilometers to that hiding place in my town and I told them what was going on. The following evening, when it got dark, my uncle who was now with me, said he knew this farmer several kilometers away from our town. We went there to him and he took us in.

The farmer took us in for three months and he fed us, but he couldn't keep us forever. Nobody knew how long this war was going to take—a month or two, or three, or six.

After this, we kept going to the same places. We didn't know what to do. We decided to go to a civilian German that I knew very well and I had worked for him before. I managed to go to him and I talked to him.

I knocked on his door in the evening, and when he saw me, he was very much surprised where I came from and how I had managed to survive. He thought I was dead, because he had heard the whole thing, the shootings.

Well, he did register all of us and we went back to work. He had some more Jewish people working in our city *Jedlińsk*, in the back, by the river. They were working on the land and I started to work for him again. It was going on for several months.

They put us to work in the field. They called it *Landeswirtschaft*, (people who work the land). There they grew food in the summer, potatoes and all other kinds of vegetables.

There we worked and there I got in my uncle and two other guys who were brothers. It was a little camp, not a concentration camp, where you worked with the farmers on the land. We worked there about eight months. Then, the same thing happened over there. We were surrounded by the Gestapo and SS, and {*stops to emit a large sigh*} we got scared that the same thing shouldn't happen as before.

One German, who was a civilian, assured us on the loudspeaker that nothing was going to happen to us. His name was Braun, a nice man who didn't hurt anyone. He said they were going to take us in the morning to an ammunition factory called Pionki.

That was the only gunpowder factory in Poland and it happened exactly as the Germans told us. They didn't hurt us and we could take as little as we had with us on the truck.

CHAPTER TEN

Pionki

Pionki is a town in Radom County, Poland surrounded by the Kozienice Wilderness, now a national forest preserve. It is located twelve miles from Radom and sixty-five miles from Warsaw. Originally, it had an arms factory, which manufactured explosives, and its location was deliberate among the forests and swamps of the Kozienice Wilderness. This location took it away from main population centers and along the strategic rail line Radom–Deblin. The Pionki factory became a German slave labor camp during World War II that produced gun powder for the German war effort. A new factory exists today making different products such as plastics, along with gun powder.

They put us on the trucks to Pionki. There, it looked pretty grim, pretty bad. There were quite a few rows of barbed wire all around the factory. In my mind was going around how to escape from there—because I kept escaping from everywhere—but here it did not look that great.

Pionki was a large place, made into a slave labor camp, well-guarded and surrounded by barbed wire. This was in the spring of 1942.

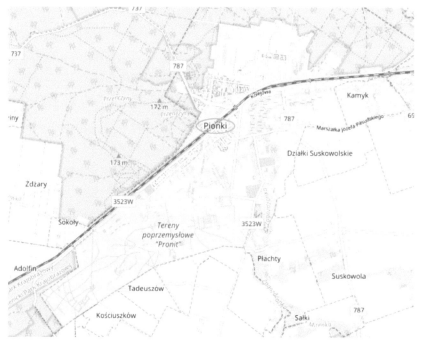

Map of Pionki.

So, I kept my eyes open, and the next day, we were assigned to work. My work was to help unload the coals. It was called the powerhouse. The section that we were assigned to work in was called *haufcolonie*, the shipping section.

Whenever the trains came in with coals, there could be eight to twelve railroad cars, in daytime or night time. It made no difference. There were so many guys, eighty or ninety, and we had to unload the coal from the railroad cars. There were two fellows to one car. There had to be an emptier. Once the car was unloaded, we could sit down and rest or they would take us back. We had to walk about four kilometers to go back to the barracks until the next day.

Old munitions factory in Pionki.

One day, a guard came from another department where they made gunpowder, and he said he needed four volunteers. I lifted my hand up. I went with a couple of boys and it was much, much better there for me.

They put me in with another guy, and we made four sacks of paper. It had to be dumped into one of those mixers. Then nitroglycerin was added. You pressed the button.

There was a little building in the back. There was a Jewish girl sitting, watching. They knew how much paper we ran. You had to start the spinners, it ran on a belt. If a guy did not know what to do, and turned the wheel too quickly, the belt slipped off. If it did, it took a half an hour to fix. I had a guy with me and we both did pretty well. Every fifteen minutes you had to make one of those measurements.

There was a blackboard where you wrote down—9:00 to 9:15—taken out. Everything was open. You took it out from the spinner, it was like a cake, and you put it on the cart. Later, kids came and pushed it away and they brought you more of that paper.

Every day, you had to make 24 more of them. Every 15 minutes you would make one, so you should make four of them in an hour. Most of the workers couldn't make it.

One day, one of the Germans came in and took a chair and sat down to see how we worked. The German said, "From now on you are going to get rubber uniforms," because the water was *spritzing* (splashing) out everywhere. He also said, "Both of you are going to get double soups!" He could see we were doing it and the others could not do it. But, we made trouble for the other guys.

Soon we got an idea. We started putting in three times as much nitro as we were told. We knew that when they made bullets out of this that it would make the gun explode. We made this sabotage whenever we could. But we couldn't do this too long because the Germans would know it was us. We would have to get out of there.

I was about fourteen and a half. I was only there for three or four weeks and I was thinking about escaping. Yet, I was scared to go alone because this was a different story now. We were in a different place in the forest and I was a little bit afraid to go alone.

After being there awhile, I met with different fellows. We decided this one night to meet at a certain point because there were different sections of work. All of us worked in different sections, and all of it was through barbed wire.

You couldn't go from one section to the next without going through a *portiere* (door). You had to go through the Ukrainians or the Germans to a certain place. You couldn't just walk in and say "Here I am." They wouldn't just let you go through. If you did, you would be in big trouble.

We were supposed to meet at this one point at one o'clock in the morning when it was dark. For some reason that night, I couldn't go because they sent me to bring food from the kitchen to two guys. This one German went with us and there was no way I could get away. And they didn't wait for me and they escaped. They got out.

But when they got out, they were caught—all of them. There were seven or eight, I don't remember exactly. The guards brought them in and the next day they were all hanged, one by one. And we all had to stay and watch and see the whole thing.

Even that didn't stop me. I made up my mind that I was going to escape no matter what, even if the same thing happened to me.

After a few days, I decided that I didn't want to go with a large group anymore. So, I did find somebody from my town, Jedliński. This fellow, who escaped with me was a little bit older. He was my neighbor who lived next door. He was a married man with two children. He had already lost his wife and the two children to Treblinka. So, he was alone and both of us decided to escape.

We met at about six o'clock in the summer evening, and we were hiding for another two hours under the boxes where they put the gunpowder. There were a lot of boxes and we were hiding there instead of going back to our barracks. We were hiding there until dark fell. We were hiding there the whole night and the next day and all night.

We could hear Germans and Ukrainians talking there. We were lying there quietly. We had enough food to last a couple of days. The next day, we escaped late in the afternoon, just before it got dark.

When it started to get dark, we both crawled to the fence. We had wire cutters and we cut the wire and we crawled through. Then we crawled slowly to another place where there were wires again and we kept on moving forwards. We had to do it six or seven times before we were able to get out.

When we got out, you could see the night start to get a little darker, night was falling and we got out. Then, I don't know where they came from, but suddenly, we were caught!

CHAPTER ELEVEN

The Getaway

There were two Germans and one Pole. I was very young and the other guy was older and they thought he had a lot of money which he probably had some with him. The two Germans did not want the Pole to see them take the money away from him, so they took my friend away on the side.

That Pole was holding me tight, under the collar of my jacket and that Pole asked me if I had money. He was an older man. I could smell that he was drunk. I could smell the whiskey on him and I told him I had a little bit of money. I took my billfold out and when I took my billfold out, he let me loose. And when he let me loose, I kicked him a couple of times and he fell over right away. I kicked him with my foot on both sides. I felt I killed him, I don't know. I beat him up pretty good, and I ran away.

When I started to run a minute or two, I was running closer to the forest. The heavy forest was about a quarter mile away. I tried to make it immediately to that forest, but after running a minute or two or three, I could hear the bullets falling right in front of me. The Germans realized what happened and they were shooting after me.

But I was running kind of zigzag—right to left and left to right and I fell down and got up and I managed to come to the forest in a very short time. It was starting to get too dark. They didn't run after me. They were just shooting some bullets.

My heart was beating very, very loud. I could still feel it today. I could hear it going BOOM, BOOM, BOOM.

CHAPTER TWELVE

Alone in the Forest

When I got to the forest, the night fell and it started to rain a little bit. So I didn't run deep into the forest. I sat down right by the edge, by a tree, and my heart was beating very hard. I had an apple in my pocket and I bit into the apple a little bit, because my throat was dry. I took some leaves, dripping a little because they were wet. I lay quietly.

After a while, night fell and I could see the lights and candle lights going on in the windows of the farmers and I could hear some dogs barking. *I was alone.*

After a little while, I could hear every once in a while a scream. I realized right away this had to be my friend, Liebka, and I realized he is yelling and yelling.

Lying there thinking, there in the forest, I couldn't think of anything else. And I figured that I am the only one who could help him, because I figured that the Germans tied up his legs and his hands and he is lying there. This is what went through my mind at that time. I figured I am the only one who can help him now.

So I slowly crawled back inch by inch. It took me a little while. When I got back it was already dark and I could only go back to the same place where he was by his motions, by his screaming once in a while, by his sound.

When I got to him, he wasn't tied up with any rope. He was stabbed by a bayonet several times from the Germans. I pulled his legs apart, they were not tied, and his hands apart, they were not tied. I felt the blood all over.

While I was there and saw him, I got very wild and started to run and instead to run to the forest, I ran back to the barbed wire. I cut myself pretty badly. I scratched my hands and my face very badly. Realizing what I had done, I turned around back to the direction of the forest. I started to run a different way.

I was running into the forest, I don't know how long. I ran and ran. I don't know if I ran ten miles or fifteen. I just kept running and running until I fell asleep in the forest. But when I woke up, it was almost a day gone. I must have fallen down and fallen asleep for a whole day. I was knocked out.

When I woke up, it was dark again and I wanted to get away. I kept walking and running, and running and walking for most of the night until I got tired again, because I wanted to get as far away from that place, Pionki, as possible. I couldn't go anymore. I had no idea where I was.

I kept running all day, and I did find blackberries that you find in the forest. I sat down and I ate those berries for an hour at least, the *big* blackberries. I found mushrooms and I ate some raw mushrooms.

CHAPTER THIRTEEN

No Longer Alone

The third day, I realized that there is someone else in the forest. Slowly and quietly, I could hear some kind of noises. I saw livestock, cows and horses, and I realized there is another young kid over there with the horses and cows.

I walked over to him, realizing that what happened was he was hiding livestock from the Germans. The livestock was from the village close by. The Germans took away all the livestock they could from the Polish farmers.

I went over to him and I talked to him. He asked me right away if I was Jewish and I said, "yes". I told him I escaped from a camp.

He had all kinds of food. He had bread and milk from the cows and we had like a picnic. He cut me a big slice of bread. Then he got milk from the cow. We were eating and drinking and it was very nice.

We burned a fire and cooked some potatoes. We were together and at least I was not alone. I wasn't afraid of him. He was hiding from the Germans, too.

After being with him a few days, he told me that in the next village there is an old Polish man. He said a Jewish guy came every Wednesday and the Polish old man gave him food. I wasn't sure if this was a trick or if this is really the truth. But, I decided to take a chance, to go on Wednesday down there before it got dark. I would go to that farmer and see if the Jewish guy actually comes there.

Sure enough, I came up to that farmer and talked to him. I told him I am Jewish and he said that a Jewish guy is coming pretty soon and he had a bunch of food for him, some apples and beans.

I didn't know if he was telling me the truth or if he was trying to get the Germans on me. But talking to him, I realized in my heart that this is the truth. If he would have been a younger man, I wouldn't trust him at all. But an older man like this, I did trust a little bit.

Sure enough, I was sitting on the porch with that farmer and the Jewish fellow walked up. When he saw me he got scared and kept walking straight through, he didn't stop. He kept on going. That farmer said, "This is that Jewish fellow."

So, I yelled to him, *"Amkho?"* (Yiddish for 'are you a Jew?'). He turned around and kind of looked at me. He said to me, *"Amkho?"* Then he came up to me and starts to hug me and kiss me. I have never seen that man before in my entire life. He is like more than a brother, like more than a father. We were two then, not one. We spent a long time together.

The Jewish man already had a bunker in the forest. He had a lot of food saved, put away. A lot of beans because they do not spoil and some potatoes stashed away. It was a different story, like something good happened to us.

His age was maybe six or seven years older than me. He was around twenty years old. He was from Łódź, a big city. After a while, we tried to get into the Partisans and we managed to go to a place where there were a lot of them.

Becoming a Partisan

In our travels in the forest, we met some more people, some Russians. We were scared to be with the AK *(Armia Krajowa)* which is the Home Army, the resistance movement linked with the Polish government in London. Their instructions came from England. We eventually got into a group in which there were a lot of Russians, some Poles, and a lot of Jews. That's where we spent most of our time. We were in the forest hiding out until the war was over.

After we were together for a little while, my friend found out that there was a group of Partisans that were far away from that point. Through another guy, he got instructions what to do. So we had to walk for days and days and days in the forest to reach this place. This wasn't city or streets. We just had to go along in that forest, until we came to that particular place.

That forest stretched all the way through Poland into Russia and the Ukraine. It was very, very big. After so many days, we got to that place and surely we were taken by surprise. A bunch of guys with guns took us away. They took us away to a place and we were interviewed. And, they told us we were spies. They took us as spies.

This was the AK. We told them we were not spies, that we had escaped from camps, that we are Poles, also we are Jews. We were born and raised in Poland and after a lot of questions, they let us go and they took us in. But, we found out, they were just as bad as the Germans.

There were some Jewish people there, but they did terrible things to them. After deciding that this was not the place for us, one night we took off and went our own way.

We went to another group in the forest and in this group were a lot of Jewish people, a few German deserters, some Poles and a lot of Russians. The Russians were the ones taken as slaves who were in German camps. They had run away and became Partisans in the forest.

The Partisans of World War II

Throughout Nazi-occupied Europe, but especially in the forests of Poland and the Ukraine, Jewish men and women formed paramilitary resistance groups. Because they had no official status and did not keep records, it is hard to know how many there were, but estimates run from twenty to thirty thousand. Partisans were of all ages and backgrounds, both sexes, and some were even children. Some had escaped from concentration camps or ghettoes, and some had never been captured or interned. Nearly all escaped with nothing more than the clothes on their backs. Partisan groups might be just a handful of men, women and children hiding in the forest and making occasional raids, or well-organized brigades of hundreds of fighters.

Towards the end of the war many of these groups were absorbed into the advancing Soviet army.

Most partisans had no prior experience of living off the land, and they faced fearsome odds—besides being constantly hunted, they had to acquire shelter, food, clothing, weapons, and ammunition. One of the most crucial tasks was foraging for firewood. Winter weather could be just as deadly as the SS. Many partisans lived in camps or bunkers in the forests where they hunted game and gathered wild plants. Sometimes they raided German camps, and often stole from nearby farms and villages. Warm clothing taken from the bodies of dead soldiers was especially prized. Medical care was almost nonexistent, and typhoid fever—carried by lice—was common. Partisans rarely heard what was happening in the outside world; they knew only that the enemy was all around them, and that capture meant instant death. Local civilians could also be a danger—they were rewarded for turning in partisans, or killed for concealing information about them.

Those who survived to tell their stories—and many did not—usually denied that they were brave, or heroes—"we did what we had to do."

CHAPTER FIFTEEN

Life as a Partisan

As we have seen, armed resistance, which was a characteristic and to some degree new feature of the Second World War, was fundamentally different from other forms of protest against Nazi rule. Those Jews who wished to resist the Nazis with armed force had to decide with which of the often violently competing resistance movements they would ally themselves. This choice was not so difficult in the ghettos and camps, where the Jews usually had to fight alone. It was unavoidable in the forests, where partisan warfare was organized and where independent Jewish resistance was virtually impossible. It was also a decision over which the Jews had little choice, since, with some exceptions, the Home Army (Armia Krajowa, AK), not to mention the more radical Polish formations, the Lithuanian Forest Brothers (Mis ˇko broliai) and the Ukrainian Insurgent Army (Ukrayins'ka povstans'ka armiya, UPA), would not accept Jews as fighters. Among the exceptions were those Jews, like the writer Micha-Borwicz, who fought in the AK and the acculturated Jews in the AK's Information and Propaganda Bureau. A very

*small number of Jews were also absorbed into the forma-
tions of the UPA.*

I was very young so I didn't kill any Germans, but I
went out one time with a group of twelve guys at night.
We were going through two bridges. We tried to do something. I was a young kid and went along with them.

There were two things we wanted to do—we wanted
to get food and we wanted to blow up a bridge. We had
to go through this one little bridge to get to the other
one. When we got to the second bridge, one of the guys
said he saw something. He panicked. It was the Germans.
This was very close to the front line. He started to panic
and got scared and made noises. We were discovered.

The Germans started to shoot up rockets and lit up
the whole area. They were throwing up hand grenades
and I got a piece of shrapnel in my lower right leg. Then
we all started to run. I couldn't anymore. I lost so much
blood. I fell down and one of the guys picked me up and
carried me about two kilometers, which is about a mile
and a half.

In the forest, I started to feel pain and I was laying
down a little while. Then, when I could walk, they tied
my leg up and bandaged it.

After some time, it healed. I just lost a lot blood and
you could still see the mark on my lower right leg in
the front. It didn't bother me too much, only when the
weather was bad.

Polish village on edge of forest.

I was like a scout, because I was so young. I had to go out into the villages on the edge of forest to see where the Germans were. I had a pencil and piece of paper and the houses were marked by numbers on a long, long street.

On each side were homes and I had to go to a house and ask for matches. And meanwhile, I was to look around to see if the Germans were there, or no Germans were there. I had to see how many people were in the house, what kind of guns were there, if there were any machine guns and I marked it down. That was my job. It wasn't hard. It was just a little bit scary, because I was always in danger. Yet, being so young, I didn't look so suspicious. Not every day, but once in a while I had to do that.

We went out together to get food from the villages. We had to be very careful with the villagers, they were very poor. The Germans had taken away most of their food.

We had to be very careful about where to take the food. We only took food from the rich ones, those who had a lot of land.

In the daytime we were hiding. We couldn't do much. But, in the nighttime, we could take anything we wanted to. We could take anything! In the nighttime we burned fires, we were singing. We went out to the villages and brought back food. The night was ours.

When we came to a village, we went to the elder in the town, like the mayor. We told him we would be back in the next week and we had to have potatoes and flour and everything was ready for us. If not, we had to do something. We had to burn the house. A lot of farmers told the Germans about us and a lot of us (Partisans) got killed.

So we had to show our power too. Since the farmers found out something terrible could happen to them, they changed their attitude. They had the food for us.

Some of the Poles were very bad. They cooperated with the Germans. They thought the Germans were winning the war. They tried to be on the Germans' side. They had always hated the Jews. Some Jews gave them a lot of money to hide them. The Poles wanted to get rid of the Jews. So, when the Germans came, they told them about the Jews in hiding. That way, they got rid of them.

But some of the Poles helped us, because they knew they would get burned out or something would happen to them. So they cooperated pretty well. They gave us food. They did what we told them to and they did not tell the Germans anymore.

In general, I would say the Poles were just as bad as the Germans or worse. If they had been decent, a lot of Jewish people would be alive today from Poland. A lot escaped from Poland, but a lot of younger people could have been saved.

Some days, we were sitting in the forest and we were talking about when the war would be over. We were talking about survival and that we would see the day when we would have revenge, when the Germans would go down. It was part of our will to live, to tell the story.

This was our hope. We tried to save our lives. We did everything possible to salvage our lives. This kept us going daily. Every day was survival. Survival is a very powerful force.

The forest was a blessing. We could always find something to eat in the forest. It allowed us to live. But in the forest, you could also become an animal.

In the summer, it was very nice. We could get out in the fields and we could pick potatoes or anything we wanted to bring it back to the forest. We couldn't store food for a long time. It would spoil, especially bread.

We managed to get along. We could feed ourselves in the forest with mushrooms and rabbits and all kinds of things. You would be surprised what there is there. We didn't live in luxury, but we managed to live.

In our bunker in the forest, there were 11 people. After the war, they were stretched out all over the world. Several went to Israel and another man also came to Dayton. One man named Wrobel and his son were in the same bunker with me. After the war, the son went to Cuba, and the father came to Cincinnati.

Back there in the forest, the further you went, the more of us (Partisans) were in the forest. There were thousands of resistance fighters in those forests who were unspoken heroes of the war.

We could see in the end of 1943 already a change. We were brought certain news about the landing of the Americans and the Germans were losing out in Africa and the Russians started to beat them back. We could see it was only a matter of time. We were uplifted right away when the United States entered the war.

We didn't know how long it was going to take, maybe a year, or two, or three more. The communication was bad. The news didn't spread well. We had no newspaper, no messengers. The radio didn't work well.

The Poles had the same problem. They were not allowed any radios. If the Germans found a radio in a Polish house, they killed them immediately, no questions asked. It's not just that the Jews alone suffered. The Poles suffered plenty, too.

But the Jews were pointed out and they were a minority. They worked right away against them. But in the beginning, Germans killed as many Poles as they did Jews. If a Pole did something wrong, they killed him immediately. They were hung. If a German got killed, they took right away a minimum of ten people in a town or city and they could have taken twenty or thirty, too.

I felt that I was ahead of some other people when I escaped from Pionki. I escaped, I had luck. Everything I did was a little bit luck. Everything I did worked out okay.

When I escaped from Pionki into the forest, I was sitting down and talked to God. God told me what to do—to try and save my friend. I felt there is something above me that is guiding me. When I talked to God, He kind of talked back to me. I had a moment when I talked to God when He directed me at that time when I escaped from that camp and they killed the other guy.

If the Poles had been more decent, thousands could have survived. We tried to save our own lives. We did everything possible to stay alive.

Some Germans deserted the Army and came to us in the forest. They could see Germany was losing the war. And they came with machine guns and hand grenades. They came with everything. There were not a lot of them. They were fighting with the Polish underground.

The trouble with the war was it took too long—seven years. When you are in trouble, it seems like 70 years. But Hitler did not accomplish anything. He killed so many millions of people and in the end he killed himself.

Around June of 1944, the Russians reached the other side of the Vistula River. Their planes sent out leaflets to the Germans. They told them if they picked up the leaflets, this was a pass for them to freedom. We saw what was going on because we were just three or four kilometers from the Front Line.

The Russians were taunting the Germans by inviting the Germans to come over to their side. Loud speakers were set up in the forest and they told the Germans, if they didn't come, the Russians would invite themselves over to the Germans for "coffee."

That night, when the Russians came to the Vistula River, there was such turmoil. The sky was lit up and there was shooting everywhere. In our part of the forest, where we were laying, everything was lit up. The Germans were on the run from the villages and towns, because they were scared of the Russians, very much afraid. And the Germans ran into the forest. All over, there was nothing but Germans. They were hiding too, because they were afraid of the Russians. We were scared to go out of the forest that day, because the Germans were running into the forest.

This one day, the Russians didn't have far to go—twenty-five or thirty kilometers. We could see the light in the night sky from all the firing. The night was daytime. We could have gotten through, but the Russians didn't want us to come through. They wanted us to stay right where we were. They wanted us to make a little trouble. We didn't want anything to happen to us because we knew the war was almost over. That's it for us, so let us get out!

We were lying all day quietly and by the next evening, we sent out a few boys and they contacted the Russian Commandant in that village. He sent in a whole bunch of Russian soldiers back with them and they took us out of the forest. That night, we all went out. We were free!

And I remember we went in different homes where the farmers were. We were singing and dancing with the Russians and it was just wonderful.

The next day we went back to Radom. It took us most of the day to get there. As we went, we met different friends and we went back to this one big home where the German Gestapo was during the war. The Polish authorities were there and they took us in and questioned us. We stayed with them a few days and then went back to our town, *Jedliṅsk*, which was about 12 kilometers away.

There was no line anymore where the Germans were fighting, they were running. The whole thing was broken up. What happened was the Germans could see what was going on. The Russians actually stopped on the other side of the river. The Russians didn't cross and they had a good reason why they stopped. When the Polish Partisans saw the Russians were moving up closer and closer, they were almost in Warsaw. The Poles made an uprising in Warsaw.

The Partisans came from the forest and took over trains from the Germans and their trucks from the highway going to Warsaw. There were thousands and thousands of Partisans. I heard there were between twelve to fifteen thousand Partisans in Warsaw to try and help the Russians.

The Russians didn't like that. They didn't want the world to later say that the Poles had freed themselves. It was very political. So, they decided to stop. They told the Poles, "You go ahead and fight the Germans now. Why didn't you do that before when the Germans were heading towards Moscow?"

Sure enough, eleven-thirty in the night, the cannons were opened up, and everything was on fire! The Russians had the *katyushas (rockets)* on their trucks. Everything was on fire for about four to five hours. The woods were on fire, the farms were on fire and the Russians put up a tremendous fight and broke through the German lines! The Russians kept going and going and going without stopping any more, until they came to the German border. Nothing could stop them.

About four o'clock in the morning, their tanks kept going through. They took no prisoners for four days. It was unbelievable, the force, The Russian force was unbelievable. They were going day and night, and day and night.

Thousands and thousands of troops were on horses, on buggies, on tanks. It was unbelievable how many troops were going through Poland at that time. Whenever they saw Germans in uniform, they killed them. They were laying everywhere. Later on, they started to take prisoners.

When the war first broke out, some of the Polish government officials took planes and flew away to England and they ran the Underground from there. The Polish Underground was the land army.

CHAPTER SIXTEEN

Return to Jedlińsk

There were some people from my hometown not far from me in the forest, but we didn't know it. After the war was over, we came back to *Jedlińsk*. There were ten boys and one girl that came back. We lived together in what was a former Jewish home.

One of the young men with us was able to take over his father's former small butcher shop. He started to butcher cows.

Every Thursday, there was a market outdoors in my town. People came from surrounding villages and small towns. They brought cows and horses and traded everything from chickens, sheep, pigs, and butter.

It's hard to imagine what we did. I sometimes brought eight to ten cows, sheep, and calves to sell at the market. We were resourceful.

Herschel, one of our group, was very, very religious. He knew how to butcher meat so we had somewhat "kosher" meat for ourselves. He knew how to say the prayers.

We didn't do it just for ourselves. We took a horse and buggy to Radom every day or every second day, to a Christian butcher. He bought our meat and sold it and made a good living.

As for the Poles living around us, we were not in such good shape with them. During that time, after the war, they looked at us and were afraid a little bit. They could not understand how we survived. They kept their distance.

Survivors did a lot of things after the war to find out who did anything to the Jews. They took revenge. When they found out we were making trouble, the AK sent us a letter. If we didn't disappear from *Jedlińsk* in thirty days, they would kill us all. And they did things like that in Radom. We knew they could do it!

So we left our town and we all went to Germany through Czechoslovakia. We were all stateless. We each went a different direction. Some stayed in Germany a little while till they could go to Israel, some went to Brazil, and some came to the United States.

CHAPTER SEVENTEEN

From Germany to the United States

A group of survivors in Germany after the War. Anschel is second from right standing. Trying to enjoy their new found freedom.

I stayed in Germany for four and a half years. Then the couple who were next door neighbors to my family in Poland, the Weismans, found out I was alive and sent me papers in 1947 to come to Dayton, Ohio. They had come to the U.S. right before the war.

While Anschel was in Germany, he mostly socialized with other survivors as was the case for most survivors in oth-

er places. Survivors felt most comfortable with each other because other people generally didn't want to hear about the atrocities they went through. The survivors got together in groups, large or small, trying to get regain some sense of normalcy. They had lost not only their families, but also a large chunk of their young lives.

I didn't want to go to the U.S. in 1947 because I went to school in Hanover to study at the ORT Mechanics School for three years. So, I was called into Hamburg to the immigration office. I told them what was going on, and they kept renewing my papers every six months.

I finally came to the United States in October 1950 to New York and then to Dayton. When I walked in, the Weismans told me, "This is your home. You can live here as long as you want to." They gave me a room and she cooked for me. They did everything to make me comfortable.

I got a job one week later at Peffley Ford and worked three months as a mechanic. Then, three months later, I bought a truck and went

Nathan and Ethel Weisman in Dayton, Ohio. Former neighbors in Poland who brought Anschel to the U.S. in 1950.

Wedding photo.

on the road without knowing anything about the business. I wanted to work for myself. I started going to small towns and collected scrap metal from farmers and wherever else I could find. In 1953, I married Rene *(Renate)*.

Two years later, my cousin Henry, a survivor of numerous camps, came to Dayton to stay with the Weismans. Together Henry and I bought a big wrecking yard, forty—six miles from Dayton in Washington Court House, Ohio. But, I could not continue to drive back and forth.

Bert and Anschel - Father-in-law and partners for 45 years till Bert's passing.

My wife and I decided to stay in Dayton where her family lived. My wife's father, Bert, worked for an iron and metal company.

In 1955, my father-in-law and I decided to start our own scrap metal company. We each had a role in building a very successful family business.

Rene and I had four wonderful children who all graduated from very good colleges. They are all married and we have 10 grandchildren.

When the war was over, I had only one small picture of my mother. I had no picture of my father or my two sisters. I wrote to everyone I knew, cousins in Brazil and

Israel, asking if they had a picture of my parents. They all wrote back that they didn't have anything.

Rene and I finally went to visit some first cousins of my mother's in Brazil. One Friday night after dinner, we were sitting with the family and they brought me some picture albums. I looked and looked at the albums and suddenly, I was screaming, "Rene, you are not going to believe it! Here is a picture of my father." They gave me that group picture of relatives to bring home.

I feel I have left something here. But I got something back. I have a wife, kids, grandkids and a home. We have accomplished something. As long as I live here, I have *naches* (happiness). What will be—will be.

Anschel and Renate - last picture taken together.

Epilogue

Although Anschel was hesitant to speak about his Holocaust survival to most people, he did occasionally speak about it to our children as they grew up. When we got together with other survivors, those years of trauma and loss came up frequently in conversations.

I found that he felt most comfortable talking to me because I learned to listen closely and show understanding of those difficult times. I had also lost my paternal grandparents and maternal great grandmother in the Holocaust. We had similar roots and goals for our future. He, however, had the haunting memory of all his losses, of sights and sounds that no human should ever have to see, and of his many narrow escapes. Those memories always lurked in the back of his mind.

We didn't know anything about Treblinka, we didn't know about Auschwitz, we didn't know anything! We knew there were camps and that nothing good was going on there.

So, when the war was over, the survivors started to come back. But, not *anyone* from my family came back.

I don't know exactly what happened to my mother and father, or about my mother's mother (my grandmother), my two sisters. My whole family was lost. I only know they were sent to Treblinka.

Sure there is anger when you live for six years under this kind of circumstances. You have got to have some anger. There is nothing to be happy about it.

Surviving was our only hope. Someone had to live to tell what happened. Much of our survival occurred under cover of night. It shielded us. Night allowed me to escape and continue to survive. In the darkest night, I never lost hope for survival.

Yet this is a man, who in spite of everything he went through, had the resilience to create a home and a family with his wife, to raise successful children, build a thriving business and to find again his religious roots and pray with fervor. His capacity to love continued on till his untimely death at the age of seventy-six.

I went several times with my wife to speak to the kids at schools about the Holocaust. They love her, just love her. Unbelievable! No noise anywhere. A pin could drop. They can relate to her.

And the students related to him. He directed the end of his speech to the crowded auditorium full of middle school children in a small Ohio town.

You kids don't know how lucky you are to be born in the United States and to have the freedom you have. It's the most wonderful country in the world—there is nothing better.

Attributions

Maps © OpenStreetMap contributors, OpenStreetMap.org.

Descriptions and pictures of cities and towns courtesy of Wikipedia

Reference to Partisans of WWII—courtesy of Antony Polonsky's book, *The Jews in Poland and Russia*, volume 3, 1914–2008 (Oxford, 2012)

Photos of deserted Pionki factory courtesy of Julian A.

About the Author

Renate Frydman, Ph.D, has been writing since the age of eight, and worked as a contributing writer for the Dayton Daily News, a Cox newspaper, for thirty years.

She has been involved with Holocaust education and remembrance since the 1960's till the present. Renate is curator of and docent for the *Holocaust Exhibit, Prejudice & Memory* at the Museum of the U.S. Air Force in Dayton which has over a million visitors a year.

Renate is producer and interviewer for the video series, *Faces of the Holocaust*, which was produced at Wright State University in 1985 and 1995. The series is used at the U.S. Holocaust Memorial Museum and throughout the world.

She is a member of the Ohio Council on Holocaust and Genocide Education since its inception in 1986.

Renate founded the Dayton Holocaust Education Committee and Dayton Holocaust Resource Center and remains active with both. She emphasizes the harm that comes with racism and bullying in all her speeches to students.

This book, *Anschel's Story: Determined to Survive* is her tribute to the man she was married to for fifty-one years.

CPSIA information can be obtained
at www.ICGtesting.com
Printed in the USA
LVHW01n0300270118
564220LV00003B/8/P